Pebble® Bilingüe/Bilingual Plus

TODO ACERCA DEL OTOÑO/ALL ABOUT FALL

La cosecha de calabazas/ Pumpkin Harvest

Edición revisada/Revised Edition

por/by Calvin Harris

Traducción/Translation: Dr. Martín Luis Guzmán Ferrer
Editor consultor/Consulting Editor: Dra. Gail Saunders-Smith

CAPSTONE PRESS
a capstone imprint

Pebble Plus is published by Capstone Press,
1710 Roe Crest Drive, North Mankato, Minnesota 56003.
www.mycapstone.com

Copyright © 2009, 2016 by Capstone Press, a Capstone Publishers company. All rights reserved.
No part of this publication may be reproduced in whole or in part, or stored in a retrieval system, or
transmitted in any form or by any means, electronic, mechanical, photocopying, recording, or otherwise,
without written permission of the publisher. For information regarding permission, *write* to Capstone Press,
1710 Roe Crest Drive, North Mankato, Minnesota 56003.

Library of Congress Cataloging-in-Publication Data is available on the Library of Congress website.

ISBN: 978-1-5157-6181-5 (revised paperback)
ISBN: 978-1-5157-6182-2 (ebook pdf)

Editorial Credits
Sarah L. Schuette, editor; Katy Kudela, bilingual editor; Adalín Torres-Zayas, Spanish copy editor;
  Veronica Bianchini, designer; Charlene Deyle, photo researcher

Photo Credit
Capstone Press: Karon Dubke, 1, 5, 13, 15, 17, 19, 21
Dreamstime: Sandra Cunningham, cover
iStockphoto: Norbert Bieberstein, 11
Shutterstock: J. Gatherum, 9; Rob Byron, 7

Pebble Plus thanks Emma Krumbees in Belle Plaine, Minnesota, Sponsel's Minnesota Harvest in Jordan, Minnesota,
  and the Minnesota Landscape Arboretum in Chaska, Minnesota, for the use of their locations during photo shoots.

Note to Parents and Teachers

The Todo acerca del otoño/All about Fall set supports national science standards related
to changes during the seasons. This book describes and illustrates the fall pumpkin
harvest in both English and Spanish. The images support early readers in understanding
the text. The repetition of words and phrases helps early readers learn new words.
This book also introduces early readers to subject-specific vocabulary words, which are
defined in the Glossary section. Early readers may need assistance to read some words
and to use the Table of Contents, Glossary, Internet Sites, and Index sections of the book.

Printed in the United States   6000

Table of Contents

Tabla de contenidos

Fall Is Here

It's fall.

The weather outside

feels cool and crisp.

Llegó el otoño

Es otoño.

Afuera el tiempo se siente

fresco y vigorizante.

4

Orange pumpkins fill a patch of land. They grow on green vines near the ground.

Las calabazas anaranjadas llenan un trecho de campo. Éstas crecen sobre la tierra en enredaderas de color verde.

6

The vines turn brown
and dry up. It's time
to harvest the pumpkins.

Las enredaderas se van
poniendo marrones y se
secan. Llegó el momento
de cosechar las calabazas.

Picking Pumpkins

Farmers cut the ripe pumpkins from their vines.

Vamos a recoger calabazas

Los campesinos cortan las calabazas maduras de las enredaderas.

10

They set the pumpkins out
for shoppers to buy.

Colocan a las calabazas
para que los clientes
las puedan comprar.

12

Fun with Pumpkins

Pumpkins make fall a fun time. They make good heads for scarecrows.

A divertirse con las calabazas

Las calabazas hacen que el otoño sea una época divertida. Sirven para hacerle una buena cabeza al espantapájaros.

14

15

Pumpkins are
scooped out to
make jack-o-lanterns.

Las calabazas pueden
vaciarse para hacer
jack-o-lantern farolitos.

16

Pumpkins are baked
into sweet pumpkin pies.

Las calabazas se cuecen
para hacer pasteles dulces
de calabaza.

Other Signs of Fall

The pumpkin harvest has begun. What are other signs that it's fall?

Otras señales del otoño

La cosecha de calabazas ya empezó. ¿Qué otras señales hay que ya es otoño?

21

Glossary

harvest — to gather or pick crops that are ripe

jack-o-lantern — a pumpkin with a face carved into it; jack-o-lanterns are Halloween decorations.

patch — a small piece of land or field where pumpkins grow

ripe — ready to be picked or eaten

scarecrow — a figure made of straw that looks like a person; scarecrows are used to scare birds away from crops.

vine — a plant with a long stem that grows along the ground; pumpkins grow on vines.

Glosario

cosechar — recoger o juntar cultivos que están maduros

las enredaderas — planta con tallos alargado que crece cerca de la tierra; las calabazas crecen en enredaderas.

el espantapájaros — figura hecha de paja que se parece a una persona; los espantapájaros se usan para asustar a los pájaros y alejarlos de los cultivos.

los farolitos *jack-o-lantern* — calabaza a la que se le da forma de cabeza; los *jack-o-lantern* son adornos de *Halloween*.

maduro — listo para recogerse o comerse

el trecho — superficie pequeña de tierra o campo donde crecen las calabazas

Internet Sites

FactHound offers a safe, fun way to find educator-approved Internet sites related to this book.

Here's what you do:

1. Visit *www.facthound.com*
2. Choose your grade level.
3. Begin your search.

This book's ID number is 9781429632621.

FactHound will fetch the best sites for you!

Index

Sitios de Internet

FactHound te brinda una forma segura y divertida de encontrar sitios de Internet relacionados con este libro y aprobados por docentes.

Lo haces así:

1. Visita *www.facthound.com*
2. Selecciona tu grado escolar.
3. Comienza tu búsqueda.

El número de identificación de este libro es 9781429632621.

¡FactHound buscará los mejores sitios para ti!

Índice